# Zermatt Hiking Guide 2025

A New Pocket  Adventures Guide in the
Heart of the Swiss Alps

Jane Doe

**Disclaimer**

The information in this book is intended as a guide for adventure travelers and hikers in Zermatt and the surrounding areas. While every effort has been made to ensure accuracy and up-to-date details, the author and publisher do not take responsibility for any changes, errors, or omissions that may occur after publication. Travelers should always verify details such as permits, weather conditions, and local regulations before embarking on their journey. Adventure activities carry inherent risks, and readers are encouraged to exercise caution, consult with local experts, and take necessary precautions for their safety.

# Table Of Contents

**INTRODUCTIONS**..............................................................5

    Preparation and Safety........................................... 14

**BEGINNERS TRAILS**..................................................... 21

    Five Lakes Walk (Leisee, Stellisee, Grindjisee, Moosjisee, Mosjesee)............................................ 21

    Gorner Gorge Adventure.................................... 26

    Sunnegga Paradise Loop..................................... 32

**INTERMEDIATE TRAILS**.............................................. 38

    Riffelberg Trail...................................................... 38

    The Matterhorn Glacier Trail.............................. 43

    Patrouille des Glaciers Path............................... 50

**ADVANCED TRAILS**...................................................... 55

    The Haute Route to Chamonix............................ 55

    The Monte Rosa Tour.......................................... 60

    The Breithorn Crossing....................................... 66

**FAMILY-FRIENDLY ADVENTURE**................................ 73

    Zermatt's Storybook Trails for Kids.................... 73

**CULTURAL AND HISTORICAL SITES**...................... 81

    The Matterhorn Museum - Zermatlantis.............. 81

    The Old Village of Zermatt.................................. 84

    Mountaineer's Cemetery...................................... 85

**DINING AND ACCOMMODATION**.............................. 88

    Mountain Huts and Their Histories...................... 88

**SEASONAL ACTIVITIES AND EVENTS**..................... 96

**DAY TRIPS FROM ZERMATT**................................... 103

Saas-Fee...............................................................103

Montreux..............................................................104

The Aletsch Glacier............................................105

Brig.......................................................................105

Combining Hiking with Other Activities in Zermatt107

**SUSTAINABLE TOURISM PRACTICES...................120**

# INTRODUCTIONS

Nestled in the southern reaches of Switzerland's Valais canton, Zermatt stands as a jewel of alpine adventure, attracting visitors from across the globe with its stunning landscapes and the iconic silhouette of the Matterhorn. This car-free village offers a blend of rustic charm and upscale amenities, making it an ideal getaway for nature lovers and thrill-seekers alike.

Zermatt's origin as a humble farming community is still visible in its historic center, where old barns and granaries stand preserved amidst luxury boutiques and gourmet restaurants. The transformation began in the mid-19th century when the allure of the Alps drew the first wave of mountaineers. The successful ascent of the Matterhorn in 1865 marked Zermatt as a mountaineering mecca, a status it retains to this day.

Accessibility is a key feature of Zermatt, despite its remote location. Trains from Täsch transport visitors into the heart of the village, ensuring a peaceful, exhaust-free environment. This commitment to sustainability enhances the pristine quality of the air and contributes to the clarity of the alpine light, casting the surrounding peaks in spectacular relief.

The cultural fabric of Zermatt is woven with traditions of the Valais region, from the distinct melodies of Alphorn players to the savory delights of raclette and fondue. The village hosts several annual events that showcase its heritage, including the Zermatt Unplugged music festival and the Patrouille des Glaciers ski mountaineering race.

In terms of hiking, Zermatt offers routes for all levels of experience. Trails like the Five Lakes Walk provide panoramic views and the chance to see the Matterhorn reflecting in tranquil waters, while the more challenging Haute Route extends towards Chamonix, offering a multi-day trek through some of Europe's most breathtaking scenery.

Zermatt remains at the forefront of alpine tourism not only for its scenic beauty but also for its innovative approach to resort management. The introduction of solar-powered transport and efforts to reduce carbon emissions are part of its commitment to preserving the natural environment that makes it so special. For visitors, Zermatt represents not just a place to visit but a chance to engage deeply with the natural world, challenging themselves physically while rejuvenating spiritually in the heart of the Swiss Alps.

## Understanding Zermatt's Unique Geography

Zermatt's unique geography is a tapestry of dramatic landscapes, dominated by the towering presence of the Matterhorn, one of the most famous peaks in the world. Situated at the southern tip of Switzerland's Valais canton, Zermatt is encircled by a crown of 38 four-thousander peaks, offering an unparalleled vista of the Swiss Alps. The town itself lies at an altitude of about 1,600 meters (5,250 feet), providing a natural balcony from which to observe the splendor of the surrounding mountains.

The area is defined by its alpine climate and topography, which include vast glaciers, rugged rock faces, and verdant valleys. The Gorner Glacier, second only to the Aletsch Glacier in size within the Alps, is particularly noteworthy.

This ice giant is a stark reminder of the glacial forces that have shaped the region over millennia, carving out deep valleys and depositing moraines that speak to the Earth's ancient past.

Zermatt's location makes it a nexus for geological and climatic research, particularly concerning glaciology and alpine ecosystems. Scientists and researchers are drawn to the area to study the impacts of climate change on the alps, which are visible in the retreating glaciers and shifting snow lines. This scientific interest adds another layer to the region's appeal, making it a hub for educational tourism aswell as recreational activities.

Hydrography plays a critical role in Zermatt's geography as well. The region is rich in water resources, fed by meltwater from glaciers. This abundance is crucial not only for the local ecosystem but also for hydropower, which is a significant source of renewable energy for the area. Streams and rivers, such as the Matter

Vispa, course through the landscape, supporting both human and wildlife populations.

Zermatt's commitment to preserving its unique geography is evident in its sustainable tourism practices. The town has implemented stringent policies to maintain air quality and reduce environmental impact, including the prohibition of combustion-engine vehicles. Electric taxis, buses, and private vehicles are a common sight, ensuring that the area remains pristine and its air pure.

For hikers and nature lovers, Zermatt offers a gateway to explore an environment where nature's power and fragility are on full display. From the challenging trails that ascend to breathtaking viewpoints to the accessible walks through alpine meadows, the geography of Zermatt provides a diverse range of outdoor activities that allow visitors to connect deeply with the natural world. This unique combination of natural beauty, scientific interest, and sustainable practices makes Zermatt not just a destination, but a profound experience for those who visit.

## Local Customs and Culture

Zermatt, a village steeped in tradition, mirrors the rich heritage of the Valais region. Its customs and culture are a vibrant tapestry of old-world charm and contemporary Swiss lifestyle, providing a unique glimpse into the life of the alpine communities. One of the most iconic elements of Zermatt's cultural landscape is the practice of Alphorn blowing, an ancient form of communication now celebrated as a musical art form, particularly during the Zermatt Folklore Festival which attracts performers and audiences from across Switzerland.

Culinary traditions also hold a special place in the daily life of Zermatt. The local cuisine is renowned for its emphasis on simplicity and flavor, featuring ingredients like cheese, potatoes, and dried meats. Dishes such as raclette and fondue offer a taste of the communal spirit that defines Swiss dining, bringing people together to share a meal after a day in the mountains.

Zermatt's respect for its environment is evident in its sustainable practices. The village promotes eco-friendly tourism, ensuring that its natural beauty and cultural heritage will be preserved for future generations. This deep-rooted appreciation for nature and community is reflected in the warm hospitality extended to visitors, making Zermatt a truly welcoming destination.

# Preparation and Safety

Embarking on a hiking adventure in Zermatt requires thoughtful preparation and an awareness of the unique environmental conditions you may encounter. Ensuring you are well-prepared with the right gear and knowledge of safety protocols can significantly enhance your experience and safety.

### Essential Gear and Clothing

The right gear is essential for a successful and safe hiking trip in Zermatt. Depending on the duration and difficulty of your hike, your backpack should include:

**Footwear:** Waterproof hiking boots with good ankle support and grip are essential, as the terrain can vary from muddy paths to rocky inclines. **Clothing:** Layering is key in the alpine climate. Start with a moisture-wicking base layer, add an insulating layer, and top it with a waterproof and windproof jacket. Weather in the mountains can change rapidly, and proper clothing is crucial.

**Navigation Tools**: A map, compass, and GPS device are vital, even on well-marked trails. Zermatt's topography can be challenging, and fog or a sudden storm can disorient even experienced hikers. **Headgear and Gloves**: A warm hat and gloves are necessary for higher altitudes where temperatures can drop significantly, even in summer.

**Sunglasses and Sunscreen**: UV radiation is more intense at high elevations, making good sunglasses and high SPF sunscreen essential.

Hydration and Food: Carry enough water and snacks like nuts, dried fruit, and energy bars. Consider a portable water filter for longer treks where water sources are available.

**First Aid Kit**: Include basic supplies such as bandages, antiseptic wipes, blister prevention pads, and medications for common ailments like headaches and nausea.

Multi-tool and Repair Kits: Useful for gear repair and unexpected situations. **Lighting**: A headlamp or flashlight with extra batteries is crucial if you find yourself on the trail after dark.

**Weather and Seasonal Considerations**
Zermatt's weather can be unpredictable, and hikers should be prepared for all conditions:

**Summer (June to September):** The most popular hiking season offers warm weather and blooming flora. However, afternoon thunderstorms are common and can be dangerous.

**Fall (October to November):** Cooler temperatures and fewer crowds make fall a great time for hiking. Be prepared for early snowfalls at higher elevations.

**Winter (December to March):** Winter hiking in Zermatt is limited to lower altitudes or well-prepared trails as snow and ice cover most paths. Avalanche risk is significant, and proper winter gear, including crampons and ice axes, may be necessary.

**Spring (April to May):** This season sees melting snow and reemerging trails. Hikers need to be cautious of unstable paths and leftover ice.

**Safety Tips**

Check the Weather: Before setting out, check the local weather conditions. Zermatt Tourism and local weather stations provide updates.

Inform Someone: Always let someone know your planned route and expected return time.

Stay on Marked Trails: Zermatt's trails are well-marked, but straying from them can increase your risk of getting lost or encountering dangerous terrain.

Respect Wildlife: The area is home to diverse wildlife, including ibex, marmots, and birds. Keep a safe distance and do not feed the animals.

Be Avalanche Aware: Learn about avalanche risks if hiking in winter or spring. Consider carrying avalanche safety equipment such as a beacon, probe, and shovel if venturing into areas where avalanches are a risk.

## Emergency Contacts

In case of an emergency, it's vital to know whom to contact:

Rega (Swiss Air Rescue): Dial 1414 for emergency air rescue. Rega operates helicopters equipped for mountain rescues. **European Emergency Number**: Dial 112 anywhere in Europe for emergency services.

Local Mountain Rescue Services: Keep the contact information for Zermatt's mountain rescue teams on your person at all times.
Zermatt Tourism Office: They can provide assistance and information on local conditions and safety updates.

Preparing adequately for a hike in Zermatt by understanding the essential gear, weather considerations, and safety tips can make the difference between a memorable adventure and a perilous ordeal. Always prioritize safety and respect the natural environment to ensure a sustainable and enjoyable experience for all.

# BEGINNERS TRAILS

## Five Lakes Walk (Leisee, Stellisee, Grindjisee, Moosjisee, Mosjesee)

The Five Lakes Walk (5-Seenweg) in Zermatt is an ideal trail for beginners, offering stunning views of the Matterhorn and a gentle introduction to hiking in the Swiss Alps. This scenic route encompasses five beautiful lakes — Leisee, Stellisee, Grindjisee, Moosjisee, and Mosjesee — each offering unique views and a peaceful environment. The trail is not only popular for its picturesque landscapes but also for its accessibility and the relatively easy terrain that makes it suitable for families and less experienced hikers.

**Trail Overview**

Length: Approximately 9.3 kilometers (5.8 miles)

Elevation Gain: About 286 meters (938 feet)

Difficulty: Easy

Starting Point: Sunnegga

Ending Point: Blauherd

Duration: Typically 2.5 to 3.5 hours

## Description

**Leisee:** The first lake on the route, Leisee, is perfect for families. It offers excellent facilities including picnic areas, a playground, and a swimming area where children can play while adults enjoy the spectacular view of the Matterhorn. The lake is reached from Sunnegga via a funicular, making it easily accessible.

**Stellisee:** A bit further along the trail, Stellisee is famous for its reflective view of the Matterhorn. It's one of the most photographed spots in Zermatt. The lake's surface mirrors the towering mountain, providing a perfect backdrop for memorable photos. Fishing enthusiasts can also try their luck here as the lake is populated with trout.

**Grindjisee:** Known for its tranquil setting surrounded by alpine flora, Grindjisee offers a serene stop along the hike. This lake is less crowded and provides a more secluded atmosphere for hikers wanting to enjoy the sounds of nature.

**Moosjisee:** Continuing the hike, Moosjisee stands out due to its unusual color — a result of the mineral deposits in the water. The lake is a recent addition to the landscape, created by damming for hydroelectric power. Despite its functional origin, it has become a scenic highlight on the trail.

**Mosjesee:** The final lake, Mosjesee, is the highest point of the hike. Often less visited due to its more remote location, it offers a quiet retreat with fewer tourists and pristine natural beauty.

## Route Directions and Tips

The trail is well-marked and can be started from Sunnegga, where a funicular ride from Zermatt drops you at the start. From Sunnegga, you hike uphill to Leisee, then follow the signs leading to Stellisee. The path to Grindjisee diverges slightly but remains clear and manageable. After visiting Moosjisee and Mosjesee, you can descend to Blauherd, where a cable car can take you back to Zermatt.

It's advisable to wear good hiking shoes as the paths, though not steep, include rocky and uneven sections. Also, carrying a light backpack with water, snacks, and a basic first aid kit is recommended. The trail is most enjoyable from June to September when the weather is warmer and the paths are clear of snow.

The Five Lakes Walk is a perfect introduction to the alpine beauty surrounding Zermatt, offering easy hiking with minimal elevation gains and spectacular views. Each lake along the trail has its own charm, making this hike a delightful experience for beginners or those looking for a leisurely day out in nature.

## Gorner Gorge Adventure

The Gorner Gorge, located just a short distance from the heart of Zermatt, offers an exhilarating and unique adventure for visitors of all ages. Carved by the Gornera River over thousands of years, this natural wonder is a spectacle of sculpted rocks and swirling waters, creating an otherworldly landscape that is both awe-inspiring and accessible.

**Trail Overview**

Length: Approximately 2.5 kilometers (1.55 miles) round trip

Elevation Gain: Minimal, as the trail mainly follows the river level

Difficulty: Moderate, due to the nature of the walkways and steps

Starting and Ending Point: South of Zermatt near the end of the Gorner Gorge via a marked path from the village

Duration: About 1 to 1.5 hours

**Description**

The Gorner Gorge adventure begins just south of Zermatt. The access is well-marked and leads adventurers to a small entrance fee booth, where a nominal charge contributes to the maintenance and safety of the facilities. From the entrance, the trail descends into the gorge itself, where the temperature drops and the sound of rushing water dominates the senses.

As you enter the Gorner Gorge, the environment changes dramatically. The cliffs tower above, ranging from 20 to several hundred feet in height, showcasing striations and patterns that tell the geological history of the area. The path, secured with metal walkways and bridges, winds along the river, allowing for safe exploration of this dynamic environment.

The gorge is a masterpiece of natural art, with vibrant green mosses contrasting against the dark, wet stones, and the river's icy blue waters cutting through the landscape. Sunlight filters down in beams, illuminating the mist that rises from the churning water, creating an ethereal atmosphere.

**Safety and Accessibility**

The walk through Gorner Gorge is secured with handrails and reinforced pathways, making it accessible to most visitors. However, it is recommended that hikers wear sturdy shoes as the paths can be slippery, especially when wet. It's also advisable to bring a waterproof jacket, as the spray from the river can reach the walkways.

One of the highlights of the Gorner Gorge adventure is the series of waterfalls that cascade down into the river below. These provide not only a stunning visual spectacle but also a refreshing coolness that enhances the experience. Informational plaques along the route offer insights into the

formation of the gorge, the local flora and fauna, and the hydrological cycle that impacts the region.

For those looking for a more adrenaline-pumping experience, the gorge is also a popular spot for fixed rope routes (via ferrata) and rock climbing. These activities offer a hands-on way to engage with the unique geology of the gorge and are guided by local experts who ensure safety and provide equipment.

**Environmental Considerations**

The preservation of Gorner Gorge is a priority for the Zermatt community. The area is maintained with an emphasis on sustainability and minimal environmental impact. Visitors are encouraged to respect the natural habitat by staying on designated paths and disposing of trash properly. The gorge also serves as an educational site, where people can learn about the importance of natural conservation and the specific environmental challenges faced by mountainous regions.

The Gorner Gorge provides a captivating escape into a natural phenomenon that is both ancient and dynamic. The combination of easy access, moderate hiking difficulty, and the dramatic beauty of the gorge makes it a must-visit destination for those traveling to Zermatt.

This adventure not only connects you with the power of nature but also leaves you with a deeper appreciation for the delicate balance of these incredible landscapes.

# Sunnegga Paradise Loop

Nestled in the heart of the Swiss Alps, the Sunnegga Paradise Loop is an idyllic hiking trail that offers panoramic views of the Matterhorn and a peaceful escape into nature. This loop is perfect for families, photographers, and casual hikers looking to experience the beauty of Zermatt without venturing into more challenging alpine terrain.

**Trail Overview**
Length: Approximately 7 kilometers (4.3 miles)
Elevation Gain: About 230 meters (755 feet)
Difficulty: Easy to moderate
Starting and Ending Point: Sunnegga Station
Duration: About 2 to 3 hours

**Description**
The journey begins with a ride on the Sunnegga funicular, an underground railway that swiftly climbs through the mountain, delivering hikers to Sunnegga Station at an altitude of 2,288 meters (7,507 feet). From here, the trail gently

unfolds, offering immediate views of the surrounding peaks.

As you embark on the Sunnegga Paradise Loop, the path leads you through a varied landscape of lush meadows, dense forests, and alpine lakes. The trail is well-marked and maintained, making it accessible for even novice hikers. The gentle inclines and occasional flat stretches allow for a leisurely pace, perfect for soaking in the vistas and the tranquil mountain atmosphere.

**Lake Leisee:** One of the first highlights along the loop is Lake Leisee, a favorite spot for families. The lake has a picnic area, playground, and a swimming area where children can splash around on warm days. The clear waters reflect the Matterhorn, offering one of the most iconic views in Zermatt.

**Marmot Watching**: The Sunnegga area is known for its population of marmots. These friendly alpine creatures can often be seen sunning themselves on rocks or bustling through the undergrowth. Informational signs provide insights into their habits and role in the ecosystem.

**Flower Trails**: Depending on the season, the loop is adorned with a burst of wildflowers. Botanical enthusiasts will appreciate the variety of species that thrive at this altitude, including alpine roses, edelweiss, and gentians.

**Rest Stops and Restaurants:** Strategically placed benches and rest stops offer places to unwind and enjoy the scenery. Additionally, several mountain restaurants along the route serve traditional Swiss cuisine, making them perfect stops for a scenic meal or refreshment.

### Safety and Accessibility

The Sunnegga Paradise Loop is designed to be accessible to a wide range of hikers. The trail is mostly smooth with some gravel sections and wooden walkways. It is advisable to wear comfortable hiking shoes and bring sunscreen, as the high altitude can intensify solar radiation.

Always carry water and possibly some snacks, especially when hiking with children.

Environmental and Cultural Significance
The loop not only showcases the natural beauty of Zermatt but also emphasizes the region's commitment to environmental conservation. The area is managed with a focus on sustainability, ensuring that the trails and surrounding habitats are preserved for future generations. Along the route, you may encounter signs explaining the local efforts in hydroelectric power and wildlife protection, highlighting how Zermatt balances tourism with ecological responsibility.

**Photography Opportunities**
For photography enthusiasts, the loop offers numerous opportunities to capture the majestic landscape. Early morning or late afternoon provides the best light for photography, casting the Matterhorn and surrounding peaks in dramatic relief. Reflection shots can be taken at Lake Leisee, and the diverse flora and fauna

along the trail add depth and interest to nature photography.

**Directions and Recommendations**

To reach the start of the loop, take the funicular from Zermatt to Sunnegga. The trail is circular, so you can choose to go clockwise or counterclockwise. Both directions offer unique perspectives of the landscape. The loop is best enjoyed from late spring to early autumn when the trail is free from snow and the weather is most favorable for hiking.

The Sunnegga Paradise Loop is a testament to the beauty and accessibility of the Swiss Alps. Offering a mixture of natural, cultural, and gastronomical delights, it provides a fulfilling experience for all ages and abilities. Whether you're looking for a family-friendly hike, a chance to witness alpine wildlife, or just a peaceful day in the mountains with spectacular views, the Sunnegga Paradise Loop is a perfect choice.

# INTERMEDIATE TRAILS

## Riffelberg Trail

For those ready to elevate their hiking experience beyond beginner paths, the Riffelberg Trail in Zermatt offers a splendid intermediate option. This trail is famed not only for its moderate challenge but also for its breathtaking panoramic views that encapsulate the essence of the Swiss Alps, including the magnificent Matterhorn.

**Trail Overview**
Length: Approximately 6 kilometers (3.7 miles)
Elevation Gain: About 350 meters (1,148 feet)
Difficulty: Intermediate
Starting Point: Riffelberg Station
Ending Point: Riffelalp Resort

Duration: Approximately 3 to 4 hours

## Description

The Riffelberg Trail commences at the Riffelberg station, accessible by the Gornergrat Bahn, the highest open-air railway in Europe. This convenient start point allows hikers to begin their journey at an elevation of 2,582 meters (8,471 feet), surrounded by alpine splendor.

From Riffelberg Station, the trail initially ascends gently through alpine meadows dotted with wildflowers during the spring and summer months. As you advance, the path narrows and begins a mild ascent through a larch forest, providing a shaded canopy that intermittently opens up to reveal stunning views of the surrounding peaks.

**Panoramic Vistas:** As the trail winds higher, it offers expansive views over the Gorner Glacier, the second-largest glacier in the Alps. On clear days, the vista extends across 29 peaks over

4,000 meters high, including Switzerland's highest, the Dufourspitze.

**Flora and Fauna:** This trail is a hotspot for observing high-altitude flora and fauna. Look out for the bright blooms of alpine asters and edelweiss. Wildlife sightings may include chamois, ibex, and the occasional golden eagle soaring overhead.

**Cultural Sites:** Along the route, hikers pass the Riffelberg Chapel, a picturesque small church set against the dramatic backdrop of the Matterhorn. The chapel is often open for visitors, offering a peaceful retreat for reflection.

**Geological Features:** The trail also allows hikers to experience the unique geology of the area, including rock formations and the visible effects of ancient glacial movements that have shaped the landscape over millennia.

## Safety and Accessibility

The Riffelberg Trail is well-marked and maintained, making it safe for those with some hiking experience. The elevation and uneven terrain require good quality hiking boots and perhaps trekking poles for added stability. Weather in the mountains can change swiftly, so it's wise to carry waterproof clothing and several layers to adapt to varying conditions.

## Environmental Considerations

Respect for the environment is crucial; hikers are encouraged to follow the Leave No Trace principles to minimize their impact. This includes packing out all trash, staying on marked trails to protect undergrowth and wildflowers, and keeping a respectful distance from wildlife.

For those inclined to capture the beauty of their hike, the trail provides numerous photographic opportunities. From the expansive landscapes that stretch out beneath the imposing Matterhorn to the intricate details of alpine flowers and the rugged textures of exposed rock faces, there's a wealth of subjects to explore through the lens.

## Directions and Recommendations

To access the trail, take the Gornergrat Bahn from Zermatt to the Riffelberg station. The path is clearly marked from the station and loops down towards Riffelalp, where you can either take a train back to Zermatt or continue hiking to explore further. The best time to hike this trail is from June to September when the path is mostly snow-free and the weather conditions are generally favorable.

The Riffelberg Trail offers a perfect blend of challenge and reward for intermediate hikers. With each step, the path unfolds new vistas and fresh experiences, from ethereal views to close encounters with nature. This trail not only tests your hiking abilities but also enriches your appreciation for the rugged beauty of the Swiss Alps, making it a must-visit for any enthusiast looking to step up their hiking game in Zermatt.

# The Matterhorn Glacier Trail

The Matterhorn Glacier Trail, often celebrated as one of Zermatt's most stunning hikes, offers an unparalleled opportunity to witness the grandeur of the iconic Matterhorn and the pristine alpine environment. This trail not only captivates with its majestic views but also educates hikers about the effects of climate change on the Alpine glaciers.

**Trail Overview**
Length: Approximately 6.5 kilometers (4 miles)
Elevation Gain: About 200 meters (656 feet)
Difficulty: Intermediate
Starting Point: Trockener Steg
Ending Point: Schwarzsee
Duration: About 2.5 to 3.5 hours

**Description**
The journey on the Matterhorn Glacier Trail begins at Trockener Steg, a station that can be reached via the Matterhorn Express gondola. At an elevation of 2,939 meters (9,642 feet),

Trockener Steg serves as the gateway to some of the most dramatic alpine landscapes in Switzerland.

Upon departing from Trockener Steg, the trail descends slightly to the Theodul Glacier's moraine. This section offers a palpable sense of the vast scale of glacial influence, with panoramic views of the Matterhorn's north face dominating the horizon. The path then winds along the glacier's edge, where signs of glacial retreat are evident, providing a powerful visual testament to the changing climate.

**Key Highlights**

Glacial Features: The trail offers a close-up view of crevasses, seracs, and the glacial polish on rocks, showcasing the dynamic nature of these ice giants. Information boards along the path explain the glacier's history and the ongoing impact of global warming, making this hike both a physical and educational journey.

Flora and Fauna: Despite the high-altitude and rugged terrain, the area around the trail is rich in specialized alpine flora. Bright lichens, hardy grasses, and even some blooming wildflowers add bursts of color to the rocky landscape. The skies and rock faces may also offer glimpses of mountain wildlife, including choughs, eagles, and the elusive alpine ibex.

Viewpoints: Several designated viewpoints along the trail provide breathtaking perspectives of the surrounding peaks and valleys. The most dramatic views come into play as the trail approaches Schwarzsee, revealing the Matterhorn's reflection in the dark, mirror-like waters of the lake.

## Safety and Accessibility

While the Matterhorn Glacier Trail is not technically demanding, it traverses high-altitude terrain that can be subject to sudden weather changes. Adequate preparation is essential, including warm clothing, rain gear, and sturdy hiking boots. The trail is marked but crosses rocky and potentially slippery surfaces, making trekking poles a recommended accessory for additional stability.

## Environmental Considerations

Visitors are reminded of the delicate nature of this high-altitude environment. Sticking to the trail helps prevent erosion and protects the fragile flora. As always, carrying out all trash is imperative to preserve the natural beauty and ecological integrity of the region.

Photographers will find the Matterhorn Glacier Trail particularly rewarding. Early morning or late afternoon light accentuates the rugged texture of the landscape and offers the best chances for capturing the Matterhorn without the midday glare. The interplay of light and shadow across the glacier's surface provides dramatic contrast, ideal for compelling landscape photography.

Directions and Recommendations
To reach the trailhead at Trockener Steg, take the Matterhorn Express from Zermatt. The trail ends at Schwarzsee, where you can take a cable car back to Zermatt or continue exploring other trails. The best months to hike the Matterhorn Glacier Trail are from July to September, when the path is mostly snow-free and the weather is most stable.

The Matterhorn Glacier Trail is more than just a hike; it is a journey through some of the most spectacular alpine scenery on the planet. It offers hikers a unique blend of natural beauty, geological wonder, and poignant insights into the impacts of climate change. This trail challenges the body, engages the mind, and stirs the soul, making it a must-do for anyone visiting Zermatt with a sense of adventure and a thirst for knowledge.

# Patrouille des Glaciers Path

The Patrouille des Glaciers Path is a legendary route, deeply embedded in the alpine history of Zermatt and renowned for its role in the Patrouille des Glaciers (PDG) race, one of the most challenging ski mountaineering competitions in the world. For hikers seeking to experience a part of this iconic route during the off-season, the trail offers an intense and rewarding trek through some of the most dramatic terrains in the Swiss Alps.

**Trail Overview**

Length: Approximately 53 kilometers (33 miles) when completed in full, but multiple shorter segments are accessible for hiking.

Elevation Gain: Significant, with variations depending on the chosen segment.

Difficulty: Hard

Starting Point: Varies, with one popular segment beginning at Zermatt.

Ending Point: Again, varies; the full race ends in Verbier.

Duration: Multiple days for the entire route; day trips possible for segments.

## Description

Originally designed as a military route in 1943, the Patrouille des Glaciers Path stretches from Zermatt to Verbier, crossing glaciers, rugged mountain passes, and alpine valleys. The trail is not just a physical challenge but also a journey through the breathtaking vistas that define the Valais region.

## The Hiking Experience

For those not attempting the entire route, a recommended segment starts from Zermatt and heads towards Schönbiel Hut. This section offers a manageable yet challenging hike, showcasing the diverse landscapes from lush meadows to stark glacial environments.

## Key Highlights

High Alpine Terrain: The trail traverses some of the highest and most remote parts of the Alps, providing experienced hikers with the thrill of navigating challenging terrains that include glacier crossings and steep ascents.

Historical Significance: Learning about the trail's origins, tied to the Swiss military and the annual PDG race, adds a layer of depth to the hiking experience.

Breathtaking Scenery: From the imposing Matterhorn to the distant peaks of the Pennine Alps, the vistas are unparalleled. The views of the Dent Blanche and the Weisshorn are particularly memorable.

**Safety and Accessibility**

The Patrouille des Glaciers Path is suitable for experienced hikers and mountaineers equipped with appropriate gear for high-altitude, glacier travel, including crampons and ropes where necessary. Local guides are highly recommended for those unfamiliar with the terrain. Weather conditions can change rapidly, and proper preparation is essential.

Respect for the fragile alpine environment is crucial. Hikers are urged to minimize their impact by adhering to the Leave No Trace principles. This includes planning and preparing, disposing of waste properly, respecting wildlife, and being considerate of other visitors.

For photographers, the Patrouille des Glaciers Path offers some of the most dramatic alpine imagery in Europe. The contrast between the ruggedness of the high mountains and the delicate nature of the alpine flora provides a stunning backdrop for impactful photography.

## Directions and Recommendations

Access to the trail depends on the segment chosen. For the Zermatt to Schönbiel Hut section, start from Zermatt and follow the marked trails towards the hut. This hike can be done as a long day hike or as an overnight trip, allowing for a sunrise or sunset experience in the mountains.

The Patrouille des Glaciers Path is more than just a hiking trail; it's a testament to the endurance and spirit of the alpine adventurers who traverse its length. Whether you're a seasoned hiker looking for a multi-day challenge or a photographer eager to capture the raw beauty of the Alps, this path offers a profound connection to the natural world and a deep sense of accomplishment.

# ADVANCED TRAILS

## The Haute Route to Chamonix

The Haute Route, a celebrated trek linking Zermatt and Chamonix, stands as one of the most prestigious long-distance trails in the Alps. Famed for its challenging terrain and breathtaking vistas, this route attracts seasoned hikers and mountaineers from around the world, offering an unparalleled adventure across some of the highest peaks in Europe.

**Trail Overview**
Length: Approximately 180 kilometers (112 miles)
Elevation Gain: Varies, with some sections involving significant ascents and descents
Difficulty: Hard
Starting Point: Zermatt
Ending Point: Chamonix
Duration: Typically 10 to 14 days

## Description

The Haute Route (High Route) travels through a landscape dotted with glaciers, rugged mountain passes, and picturesque alpine villages. Originating in the Swiss town of Zermatt, the trail crosses into France, culminating in the mountaineering mecca of Chamonix. This trek not only challenges the physical and mental stamina of its travelers but also rewards them with some of the most majestic scenery found in the Alps.

The journey begins in Zermatt, beneath the shadow of the Matterhorn. The initial days involve acclimatization to the high altitude and the rugged terrain. As the route progresses, hikers traverse beneath towering peaks such as Mont Collon, Pigne d'Arolla, and Mont Blanc, each offering new challenges and spectacular views.

The trail includes a mix of high mountain passes, such as the challenging Pas de Chèvres with its ladders and the Col de Riedmatten, and descents into lush valleys like the Val d'Hérens. The diversity of the landscape provides an ever-changing backdrop that keeps the journey engaging from start to finish.

## Key Highlights

Glacial Crossings: The route involves several glacier crossings, including the famous Plateau du Couloir. These segments require the use of crampons, ice axes, and ropes, as well as a knowledgeable guide for safe navigation.

Remote Mountain Huts: Along the Haute Route, there are numerous mountain huts offering basic accommodations and warm meals. These huts not only provide rest and refuge but also a chance to meet fellow trekkers from around the globe.

Iconic Landscapes: The panoramic views from cols and summits along the Haute Route are unparalleled. From these vantage points, hikers can see a horizon lined with some of the highest peaks in the Alps, including the Dent Blanche, the Grand Combin, and Mont Blanc itself.

**Safety and Accessibility**

The Haute Route is a demanding trek that requires good physical condition, mountaineering skills, and proper equipment. It is strongly recommended to undertake this hike with an experienced guide who can navigate the complex terrain and changing weather conditions. Preparation should include physical training, securing the necessary gear, and planning the trek with respect to the best season, generally from late June to early September.

Travelers are urged to practice responsible hiking by minimizing their environmental impact. This includes adhering to the principles of Leave No Trace, such as packing out all garbage, staying on designated trails to reduce erosion, and respecting wildlife habitats.

The Haute Route offers extraordinary opportunities for photography. Dramatic landscapes, the play of light on glaciers, and the rugged beauty of the Alps provide endless subjects for both amateur and professional photographers. Key photographic moments include sunrise over the peaks and capturing the ethereal beauty of the high mountain environments.

**Directions and Recommendations**

The trail can be accessed directly from Zermatt. Most hikers choose to take the route in stages, stopping overnight at various huts along the way. Booking these huts in advance is essential, particularly during the peak trekking season, as they can fill up quickly.

The Haute Route to Chamonix is more than just a hiking trail; it is a journey through the heart of the Alps that challenges the spirit and offers rewards that are not just visual but deeply personal. For those prepared to face its demands, the Haute Route presents an unforgettable adventure that epitomizes the pinnacle of alpine trekking.

# The Monte Rosa Tour

The Monte Rosa Tour encapsulates the spirit of high-alpine adventure, winding through the Swiss and Italian Alps around the majestic Monte Rosa massif, the second-highest mountain in Western Europe. This tour is celebrated not only for its stunning landscapes and challenging trails but also for its unique cross-border cultural experience.

**Trail Overview**
Length: Approximately 160 kilometers (100 miles)
Elevation Gain: Substantial, involving several passes over 2,500 meters (8,200 feet)
Difficulty: Hard
Starting and Ending Point: Typically starts and ends in Zermatt, Switzerland
Duration: Generally 8 to 10 days

## Description

The Monte Rosa Tour begins in the iconic mountain town of Zermatt, setting out towards the sprawling glaciers and rugged peaks that define the region. The route circles the massive Monte Rosa, touching parts of both Switzerland and Italy, and provides a comprehensive Alpine experience, crossing picturesque valleys, serene alpine meadows, and imposing glaciers.

From Zermatt, hikers ascend toward the Theodul Pass, the first of several high mountain passes, which offers dramatic views back towards the Matterhorn. The trail then dips into Italy, where the landscape softens into rolling alpine meadows before ascending again into the rugged high Alps.

One of the most challenging and rewarding sections of the tour is the crossing of the Monte Moro Pass, where hikers are treated to spectacular views of the Monte Rosa's eastern face. The path then leads down to the

Macugnaga, an Italian alpine village known for its deep cultural heritage and stunning scenery.

As the route curves back towards Switzerland, it passes through Saas Fee, another famous alpine resort, known for its glaciers and vibrant tourism. The final legs of the journey involve traversing several more high passes, each offering unique vistas and challenges, before descending back into Zermatt.

**Key Highlights**
Diverse Landscapes: The tour offers a variety of terrains, from rocky high-altitude trails to lush valleys filled with wildflowers, providing a full spectrum of the alpine environment.
Cultural Experience: The trail's route through both Swiss and Italian territories allows hikers to experience the distinct cultural nuances of both regions, from language and architecture to cuisine.

Glacial Encounters: The tour includes views and crossings of some of the Alps' most impressive glaciers, offering a firsthand look at these dynamic and increasingly fragile natural wonders.

## Safety and Accessibility

Given its duration and the demanding nature of its terrain, the Monte Rosa Tour is suitable for experienced hikers who are comfortable with multi-day treks in remote, high-altitude environments. Proper gear, including crampons and trekking poles, is essential, as is the ability to navigate potentially hazardous mountain weather.

Hikers are encouraged to respect the delicate alpine ecosystems by adhering to Leave No Trace principles. This includes planning and preparing to minimize impact, disposing of waste properly, and being considerate of wildlife and other hikers.

The Monte Rosa Tour is a photographer's dream, offering endless opportunities to capture the awe-inspiring beauty of the Alps. Key moments include the sunrise over Monte Rosa's snowy peaks, the dramatic landscapes from high passes, and the charming alpine villages nestled in the valleys.

## Directions and Recommendations

The tour is typically undertaken in a clockwise direction starting from Zermatt. It is advisable to plan the trip during the summer months when the passes are clear of snow and the days are longer, providing safer and more enjoyable hiking conditions.

The Monte Rosa Tour is an epic journey that challenges the body and inspires the soul. For those prepared to tackle its demands, the tour offers an in-depth exploration of the Alpine highlands, blending natural beauty with cultural richness. This route not only tests one's endurance but also rewards with unforgettable experiences and panoramic vistas that encapsulate the essence of the European Alps.

# The Breithorn Crossing

The Breithorn Crossing is a renowned high-altitude route that spans the border between Switzerland and Italy. Known for its accessible yet thrilling glacier trek, the crossing provides an excellent introduction to alpine mountaineering due to its relatively straightforward route and stunning panoramic views, including the Matterhorn.

**Trail Overview**
Length: Approximately 6 kilometers (3.7 miles)
Elevation Gain: Minimal ascent as the start and end points are at similar elevations, but the altitude itself is challenging.
Difficulty: Moderate to Hard
Starting Point: Klein Matterhorn (Switzerland)
Ending Point: Gandegg Hut or Testa Grigia (Italy)

Duration: About 3 to 5 hours

## Description

The adventure begins with a cable car ride to the Klein Matterhorn, located at an elevation of 3,883 meters (12,740 feet), making it one of the highest cable car stations in Europe. From there, the journey to the summit of the Breithorn, which stands at 4,164 meters (13,661 feet), is generally considered one of the easiest 4,000-meter peaks to ascend in the Alps due to the gradual incline and well-trodden path.

Upon departing from the Klein Matterhorn, climbers traverse the Breithorn Plateau, a vast, snowy expanse that serves as the pathway towards the peak. The climb, while not technically demanding, requires the use of crampons, ice axes, and ropes due to icy conditions and crevasses. Guided tours are highly recommended, especially for those new to glacier travel.

As hikers ascend the gently sloping ridge, they are treated to incredible views of the surrounding Alpine giants, including the Monte Rosa Massif and the Matterhorn. The summit itself offers a 360-degree panorama that encompasses many of the Alps' highest peaks.

Summit Experience: Reaching the summit of the Breithorn provides a satisfying challenge for novice mountaineers and an exhilarating experience for seasoned climbers, all within a relatively safe and manageable environment.

Alpine Flora and Fauna: While the high-altitude environment is mostly barren, the lower elevations near the start and end points can reveal diverse alpine flora and occasional sightings of wildlife such as ibex and chamois.

Photography Opportunities: The Breithorn Crossing is photogenic, offering dramatic landscapes ideal for capturing the raw beauty of the Alps. Sunrise and sunset provide particularly stunning light for photography, casting the snow and ice in hues of pink and gold.

## Safety and Accessibility

The crossing is best attempted from late spring to early autumn when the weather is most stable. Despite its reputation as an easier 4,000-meter peak, the altitude can pose a significant challenge, and altitude sickness is a risk. Adequate acclimatization, proper gear, and a guided group are recommended to ensure safety. The route is well-marked, but weather conditions can change rapidly, making it essential to be prepared for cold and wind.

Preserving the pristine nature of the Alpine environment is crucial. Climbers are urged to minimize their impact by sticking to established paths, avoiding any littering, and respecting the natural habitats encountered along the route.

## Directions and Recommendations

To access the trail, take the cable car from Zermatt to Klein Matterhorn. From the summit of the Breithorn, descend towards the Gandegg Hut or continue to Testa Grigia, where you can catch a lift back to Cervinia in Italy, making it a transnational experience.

The Breithorn Crossing offers a unique combination of accessibility and high-altitude challenge, making it an ideal venture for those looking to step into the world of mountain climbing. With its breathtaking views and manageable difficulty, it stands as a must-do for

adventure seekers and mountain enthusiasts
visiting the Zermatt area.

# FAMILY-FRIENDLY ADVENTURE

Zermatt, known globally for its iconic Matterhorn and challenging ski slopes, also offers a variety of family-friendly adventures that make it a perfect destination for visitors of all ages and abilities. From storybook trails designed to enchant the youngest hikers to accessible paths that ensure everyone can enjoy the beauty of the Alps, Zermatt caters to families looking for a memorable mountain experience.

## Zermatt's Storybook Trails for Kids

**Wolli's Adventure Park at Sunnegga**

Length: Various short loops
Elevation Gain: Minimal
Difficulty: Easy
Location: Sunnegga

One of the most beloved attractions for families in Zermatt is Wolli's Adventure Park at Sunnegga. This area is dedicated to Zermatt's famous black-nosed sheep, Wolli, and designed specifically for children. The park features interactive stations where kids can learn about the alpine environment and local wildlife through fun and engaging activities. Accessible via a funicular, the park is easy to reach and provides a safe, enclosed area where children can play and explore.

The park also includes a themed Storybook Trail, where children follow a narrative involving Wolli and his adventures around Zermatt. The trail is equipped with storyboards and playful elements that integrate the natural surroundings, making it an educational experience that sparks children's imagination and encourages a love for nature.

## Theme Paths: Marmot Trail and Adventure Forest

### Marmot Trail
Length: Approximately 3 kilometers (1.86 miles)
Elevation Gain: 100 meters (328 feet)
Difficulty: Easy
Starting Point: Blauherd
Ending Point: Sunnegga

The Marmot Trail is a fantastic way for families to observe wildlife while enjoying a gentle hike. Starting from Blauherd, the trail descends to

Sunnegga, and is well-marked and stroller-accessible, making it suitable for young children. Along the way, families can use the provided binoculars at various stations to spot marmots in their natural habitat. These playful creatures are active during the warmer months and can often be seen sunbathing or socializing.

Interpretative signs along the trail provide interesting facts about the marmots' lifestyle and their role in the ecosystem, making it both an educational and entertaining journey. The trail's gentle decline and engaging stops ensure that even the smallest hikers can enjoy the trek without fatigue.

### Adventure Forest
Length: Varies, with multiple short paths
Elevation Gain: Minimal
Difficulty: Easy
Location: Near Furi

The Adventure Forest, located near Furi, is another excellent destination for families. This area features a series of rope courses, zip lines, and bridges, designed to be safe for children while providing a thrilling experience. The courses vary in difficulty to accommodate different ages and skill levels, ensuring that every family member can participate.

The Adventure Forest also integrates educational elements about the forest ecosystem, highlighting the flora and fauna that can be found in the Swiss Alps. This blend of adventure and education makes it an ideal spot for families looking to combine fun with learning.

### Barrier-Free Trails for All Abilities

### Matterhorn Glacier Trail

Length: Approximately 6.5 kilometers (4 miles)
Elevation Gain: Minimal
Difficulty: Easy
Starting Point: Trockener Steg
Ending Point: Schwarzsee

Zermatt is also home to the Matterhorn Glacier Trail, which is designed to be barrier-free and accessible to visitors with limited mobility. This trail offers stunning views of the Matterhorn and surrounding peaks, providing a high-alpine experience that is rarely accessible for those with physical disabilities.

The trail is mostly flat and well-maintained, with a firm surface that is suitable for wheelchairs and strollers. Information panels along the route offer insights into the glacier's retreat and the geological history of the area, making it an informative journey through one of the most dramatic landscapes in the Alps.

Zermatt's family-friendly adventures provide a unique opportunity to explore the natural beauty and cultural heritage of the Swiss Alps in a way that is accessible and enjoyable for all ages and abilities. From the enchanting Storybook Trails to the exciting Adventure Forest and the inclusive Barrier-Free Trails, Zermatt ensures that every family member can participate in the wonder of outdoor exploration, making it an ideal destination for a family vacation that will be remembered for years to come.

# CULTURAL AND HISTORICAL SITES

Zermatt, nestled in the Swiss Alps, is not only a haven for skiing and mountaineering but also a rich repository of cultural and historical treasures. The town's vibrant history is encapsulated in several key locations that offer visitors a deeper understanding of the region's heritage and the pioneering spirit of its people. These sites include the Matterhorn Museum - Zermatlantis, the Old Village of Zermatt, and the Mountaineer's Cemetery, each telling a unique story of adventure, tradition, and remembrance.

## The Matterhorn Museum - Zermatlantis

The Matterhorn Museum - Zermatlantis offers an intriguing underground exhibition located in the heart of Zermatt. This museum provides a captivating insight into the historical development of the town, from its early days as a farming village to becoming one of the world's most famous mountain resorts.

## Exhibits and Features

Designed like an archaeological dig, Zermatlantis displays artifacts, photographs, and multimedia presentations that delve into the lives of the original Walser inhabitants, the development of alpine tourism, and the dramatic first ascent of the Matterhorn in 1865. One of the highlights is the re-creation of a 19th-century Zermatt village, complete with original buildings and everyday objects from the past.

Visitors can explore various thematic areas that cover aspects such as geology, flora and fauna, and the impact of climate change on the Alps. The museum also pays homage to the climbers who have attempted to conquer the Matterhorn, featuring personal items that belonged to Edward Whymper and his team, providing a poignant glimpse into their challenging expedition.

### Cultural Impact

Zermatlantis not only educates its visitors about the past but also encourages them to consider the future of mountain environments. It stands as a cultural hub in Zermatt, hosting various events, talks, and temporary exhibitions that foster a deeper appreciation and understanding of mountain culture and ecology.

## The Old Village of Zermatt

The Old Village, or "Hinterdorf," is a well-preserved part of Zermatt that dates back more than 500 years. This area contains around thirty buildings constructed in the traditional style of the Walser people, who migrated to the area in the 14th century. The houses and barns, made from larch wood and featuring stone roofs, are architectural artifacts themselves, offering a window into the harsh yet simple alpine life of earlier times.

Walking through the narrow lanes of the Old Village, visitors can see the original stadel, which are barns built on stilts with flat stones to prevent mice from getting in. These buildings, some of which have been converted into boutiques, restaurants, and residences, are characterized by their sun-beaten wood and intricately carved gables.

The Old Village is not just a tourist attraction but a living part of Zermatt, where some locals still reside, maintaining their traditions and customs. The preservation efforts are evident, ensuring that the architectural integrity and historical significance of these structures are retained for future generations to learn from and enjoy.

**Cultural Significance**

The Old Village serves as a testament to the enduring human spirit and the adaptability of the mountain people. It provides insight into the traditional construction methods adapted to the alpine climate and the community lifestyle that characterized early Swiss alpine villages.

## Mountaineer's Cemetery

The Mountaineer's Cemetery, located behind the St. Mauritius Church in Zermatt, is a solemn and reflective site dedicated to the climbers who have lost their lives on the mountains surrounding the town, including the Matterhorn.

### Graves and Memorials

Each gravesite and memorial tells a story of bravery and the ultimate sacrifice made in pursuit of conquering the Alpine peaks. The cemetery is a mix of simple crosses, elaborate tombstones, and heartfelt tributes from family and friends, commemorating lives from all over the world. Notable climbers, including members of the first ascent of the Matterhorn, are also interred here, their stories woven into the fabric of Zermatt's mountaineering legacy.

**Reflective Space**

The cemetery serves as a poignant reminder of the risks associated with mountain climbing but also as a space for contemplation and remembrance. It highlights the respect and honor the community of Zermatt holds for those who have embraced the mountains, both in life and death.

Zermatt's cultural and historical sites offer more than just a look back into the town's past; they provide a narrative of human endurance, cultural evolution, and respect for nature.

From the insightful exhibitions at the Matterhorn Museum - Zermatlantis to the historical architecture of the Old Village and the solemn remembrance at the Mountaineer's Cemetery, Zermatt showcases its heritage with dignity and pride, making these sites essential visits for anyone wanting to fully appreciate this remarkable Alpine destination.

# DINING AND ACCOMMODATION

Zermatt, a premier alpine destination, not only captivates visitors with its stunning landscapes and outdoor adventures but also offers exceptional dining and accommodation experiences. From historic mountain huts to gourmet restaurants with panoramic views, along with a diverse range of lodging options, Zermatt caters to all preferences, ensuring every aspect of your stay is memorable.

## Mountain Huts and Their Histories

Mountain huts in Zermatt are more than just places to rest; they are steeped in mountaineering history and offer unique insights into the traditional alpine way of life. These huts have been used by climbers and hikers for over a century, providing shelter and camaraderie in the remote Swiss Alps.

**Notable Huts**

**The Monte Rosa Hut** – A marvel of modern sustainable design, the new Monte Rosa Hut was opened in 2009, replacing the old hut which had served climbers since 1895. Known as the "Crystal from the Alps," it is largely self-sufficient, generating 90% of its energy from solar panels. The hut is a popular base for those attempting routes on the Monte Rosa massif.

**The Hörnli Hut** – Situated at the base of the Matterhorn on the Hörnli ridge, this hut is an iconic stop for climbers aiming to tackle the Hörnli route up the Matterhorn. Originally built in 1880, it was recently renovated to offer improved safety and comfort while maintaining its historical character.

**Fluhalp Hut** – Located at 2,620 meters, this hut offers spectacular views of the Matterhorn and the surrounding peaks. The Fluhalp Hut is known for its cozy ambiance and is accessible via a relatively easy hike, making it a favorite among families and casual hikers.

These huts not only provide practical benefits but also represent the spirit of alpine adventure, serving as communal gathering spots where stories and tips are shared between seasoned climbers and novices alike. They embody the historical and ongoing connection between humans and the mountain landscape of Zermatt.

## Gourmet Dining with Alpine Views

Zermatt's dining scene is as diverse as its landscape, featuring everything from traditional Swiss fare to sophisticated international cuisine, all served against the backdrop of the Alps.

## Top Restaurants

**Chez Vrony** – Located in Findeln, Chez Vrony offers a century-old tradition of serving organic, locally sourced cuisine. The restaurant's sun terrace provides a stunning view of the Matterhorn, making it a perfect spot for lunch during a day of skiing or hiking.

**Restaurant Zum See** – This charming restaurant is a hidden gem in the hamlet of Zum See. Known for its excellent seafood and classic Swiss dishes, it provides a quaint and intimate setting that contrasts with the grandeur of the mountains around.

**The Omnia** – With its modern twist on mountain architecture and a menu to match, The Omnia offers a fine dining experience perched above the rooftops of Zermatt. The restaurant specializes in a fusion of local and international cuisine, crafted by top chefs.

Dining in Zermatt is not just about food; it's about the experience. Many restaurants, especially those located on mountainsides, offer panoramic views that enhance the culinary journey with breathtaking vistas.

## Choosing the Right Accommodation

Zermatt offers a wide array of accommodation options to suit different tastes and budgets. Whether you prefer a luxurious hotel, a cozy chalet, or a simple room in a mountain hut, you can find the perfect place to rest and recharge.

**Luxury Hotels** – For those seeking pampering and top-notch amenities, hotels like The Zermatterhof and Mont Cervin Palace offer luxurious rooms, spa services, and gourmet restaurants. These establishments provide an elegant base from which to explore Zermatt.

**Boutique Hotels** – Smaller in scale but rich in character, boutique hotels such as the Hotel Firefly provide a more personalized experience.

These hotels often feature unique decor, attentive service, and comfortable accommodations.

**Chalets and Apartments** – Ideal for families and groups, chalets and apartments offer flexibility and privacy. Providers like Zermatt Chalets specialize in high-end chalet rentals with services that can include personal chefs and concierge services.

## Choosing Tips

When selecting accommodation, consider your priorities, such as proximity to ski lifts, views of the Matterhorn, or access to hiking trails. It's also worth considering the style of holiday you are after, whether it's a quiet retreat or being close to nightlife and restaurants. Always check recent reviews for the latest insights on service and facilities.

Zermatt's range of dining and accommodation options captures the essence of its alpine heritage while catering to modern tastes and comforts. From savoring gourmet meals amidst stunning scenery to finding a cozy spot that feels like home, Zermatt offers a perfect blend of adventure, tradition, and luxury, making every visit uniquely satisfying.

# SEASONAL ACTIVITIES AND EVENTS

Zermatt, a town that harmonizes with the seasons, offers a variety of activities and events throughout the year, catering to both the adventurous spirit and cultural enthusiast. From vibrant summer festivals to unique winter sports and spring and autumn celebrations, Zermatt provides visitors with more than just a scenic backdrop of the Matterhorn—it offers a year-round calendar packed with excitement and tradition.

## Summer Festivals and Events

One of the highlights of the Zermatt cultural calendar is the Zermatt Unplugged music festival, which takes place each April and often extends into the warmer months. This festival transforms the town into a haven for music lovers, featuring acoustic performances by internationally renowned artists as well as up-and-coming musicians. The stages are set against the dramatic alpine panorama, providing a unique concert experience that combines great music with stunning views.

### The Matterhorn Ultraks
For the sporting enthusiast, the Matterhorn Ultraks, held in August, is a series of trail running races that attract thousands of runners from around the world. The races cover several distances, challenging participants with steep ascents, rapid descents, and breathtaking landscapes. It's not just a test of endurance and speed but also a chance to experience Zermatt's trails in a competitive and communal atmosphere.

### Swiss National Day
On August 1st, Zermatt celebrates Swiss National Day with a variety of traditional festivities, including folk music, dancing, and a spectacular fireworks display. The town squares

brim with locals and tourists alike, enjoying food stalls that serve traditional Swiss fare, making it a great opportunity to engage with local culture and history.

## Winter in Zermatt: Beyond Skiing

While Zermatt is renowned for its skiing, the town offers numerous other winter activities that make it a unique destination even for those who prefer not to hit the slopes.

### Ice Skating and Curling

The natural and artificial ice rinks in Zermatt provide perfect venues for ice skating and curling. Families, couples, and groups of friends can be seen enjoying these leisurely activities, often followed by a warm drink at a nearby café.

### Winter Hiking and Snowshoeing

For those who wish to explore the mountains at a slower pace, winter hiking and snowshoeing are excellent alternatives. Zermatt boasts over 70 kilometers of groomed winter walking trails, offering serene landscapes and quiet trails covered in fresh snow. The trails are well marked and can take you from the town to secluded spots with magnificent views of the Matterhorn.

### Horu Trophy Zermatt

The Horu Trophy, one of Switzerland's largest open-air curling tournaments, takes place in Zermatt every January. This event not only draws curling enthusiasts from across Europe but also offers spectators a lively, engaging atmosphere.

## Spring and Autumn Specials

### Zermatt Food Festival

In spring, the Zermatt Food Festival is a culinary highlight, showcasing the best of local and international cuisine. Chefs from around the world gather to present their dishes, participate in cook-offs, and share their culinary expertise with visitors. This festival is a gastronomic journey that highlights innovation and tradition in cooking.

## Sheep Festival

Autumn in Zermatt is marked by the Sheep Festival, a charming event that celebrates the return of the sheep from the high alpine pastures. The festival includes a sheep parade through the main street, a sheepdog demonstration, and a competition for the best-decorated sheep. It's a family-friendly event that offers insights into the agricultural traditions of the region.

## Autumn Hiking

With the crowds of summer dissipated, autumn is an ideal time to explore Zermatt's hiking trails. The larch trees turn a golden yellow, and the clear, crisp air offers excellent conditions for photography and leisurely hikes. This season provides a tranquil atmosphere, allowing visitors to enjoy the natural beauty of Zermatt without the bustle of peak tourist seasons.

Zermatt thrives with activity all year round, offering a diverse array of events and attractions that go beyond its reputation as a skiing paradise. Each season brings its own unique charm and opportunities for visitors to immerse themselves in the local culture, sports, and natural beauty of this iconic Alpine town. Whether attending a summer music festival, participating in winter sports, or enjoying the culinary delights of the spring food festival, Zermatt provides endless possibilities for creating memorable experiences.

# DAY TRIPS FROM ZERMATT

Zermatt, nestled in the Swiss Alps, serves as an excellent base for exploring the broader Valais region and beyond. With its stunning landscapes and efficient transportation links, visitors can enjoy a variety of day trips that offer cultural enrichment, natural beauty, and historical insights. Here are some top destinations for day trips from Zermatt.

## Saas-Fee

### Explore the Glacier Village

Just a bus ride away, Saas-Fee, often referred to as the "Pearl of the Alps," is another car-free village nestled among high mountain peaks. It is renowned for its year-round ski facilities located on the glaciers, making it a perfect destination for those who wish to enjoy snow sports even in summer. The village is also home to the world's highest revolving restaurant, offering another unique viewpoint of the Alps.

## Montreux

**Jazz and Lake-Side Views**

For those willing to venture a bit further, Montreux, located on the shores of Lake Geneva, provides a stark contrast to the high alpine environment of Zermatt. Known for its mild climate and vibrant cultural scene, Montreux is famous for its annual Jazz Festival. Visitors can explore the charming lakeside promenade, visit the historic Château de Chillon, or simply enjoy the lush vineyards that surround the area. The journey involves a scenic train ride, showcasing the diverse landscapes of Switzerland.

## The Aletsch Glacier

**Witness the Largest Glacier in the Alps**

Accessible via a combination of trains and cable cars, the Aletsch Glacier is a UNESCO World Heritage site and the largest glacier in the Alps. Hiking alongside this impressive ice flow offers a humbling view of nature's power and the beauty of the high alpine environment. The region has several lookout points, such as the Eggishorn, which provides panoramic views of the glacier winding through the mountains.

# Brig

**Historical Town with Mediterranean Flair**

Close to Zermatt, Brig is a small town with a distinctly Mediterranean vibe, thanks to its sunny climate and beautiful baroque architecture. It serves as a gateway to the Simplon Pass and is ideal for exploring local history and culture. Visitors can tour the Stockalper Palace, a magnificent castle built in the 17th century, or enjoy a leisurely stroll through the old town's narrow streets.

**Italian Villages: Cervinia and Aosta**

## Cross-Border Exploration

For a taste of Italy, the nearby resort of Cervinia and the historic town of Aosta offer delightful day trips. Cervinia provides further opportunities for skiing and snowboarding, while Aosta, known for its Roman ruins and medieval monuments, offers a cultural feast. The Aosta Valley is also famous for its cuisine and fine wines, providing a perfect blend of history and gastronomy.

Zermatt's central location in the Swiss Alps makes it an ideal starting point for exploring a rich tapestry of landscapes and cultures. Whether you're ascending nearby peaks, diving into historical towns, or crossing borders, the day trips from Zermatt promise enriching experiences that complement the beauty and adventure found in the heart of the Alps. Each destination not only broadens the horizon of travel but also deepens the appreciation for the diverse offerings of the region.

# Combining Hiking with Other Activities in Zermatt

Zermatt, Switzerland, renowned for its majestic landscapes and pristine nature, offers more than just traditional hiking; it's a hub for multi-sport enthusiasts. Combining hiking with biking and paragliding in Zermatt not only amplifies the thrill but also provides unique perspectives of the Alps. Here's how adventurers can maximize their experience by blending these activities.

## Hiking and Mountain Biking

Zermatt's network of trails offers numerous opportunities for both hiking and mountain biking, making it easy to switch between the two. Many of Zermatt's trails are dual-use, meaning they are designed to be shared by hikers and bikers alike. This allows for a flexible approach to exploring the terrain—hike up to enjoy the scenery at a slower pace, then hop on a bike for an exhilarating descent.

## Sunegga to Zermatt Bike Trail

One popular route is the ride from Sunegga to Zermatt. This trail starts with a funicular ride to Sunegga, where bikers can enjoy panoramic views before beginning their descent. The route offers varied terrain, from smooth paths to challenging sections, suitable for intermediate bikers. Hikers can ascend the same path, enjoying the alpine flora and fauna, before meeting their biking counterparts for the journey back down.

## Bike Rental and Guided Tours

Zermatt is equipped with several bike rental shops that offer everything from hardtail and full-suspension mountain bikes to electric bikes, which are perfect for those who want a little extra help on the steeper climbs. For beginners, or those looking for a local's insight into the best trails, guided tours are available and can be tailored to combine hiking and biking segments.

## Hiking and Paragliding

Paragliding in Zermatt provides an unmatched aerial view of the Alps, including the iconic Matterhorn. For those looking to combine hiking and paragliding, several companies offer hikes to launch points with a flight back down to the valley. This combination not only provides the satisfaction of a hike up but also the thrilling reward of flying over the landscape you've just traversed.

## Rothorn to Zermatt Flight

A notable combo starts with a hike or a gondola ride to the Rothorn. From there, adventurers can take off with a paragliding instructor and glide over the rugged terrain, enjoying a bird's eye view of the peaks and valleys. The flight typically lands near Zermatt, offering a dramatic conclusion to an exhilarating day.

Safety is paramount in paragliding, and all flights are conducted by certified instructors. Beginners do not need any previous experience to enjoy a tandem flight, making this an accessible option for most visitors. Pre-flight briefings cover all safety aspects and ensure that participants are comfortable with the process.

## Best Time to Visit

The best months for combining these activities in Zermatt are from June to September when the weather is most favorable. Trails and paths are clear of snow, and longer daylight hours provide ample time for both hiking and biking or paragliding.

**Local Regulations and Environmental Care**

Visitors should be aware of local regulations, especially concerning trail use, to avoid conflicts between hikers and bikers. Environmental conservation is a priority in Zermatt, and all adventurers are encouraged to follow Leave No Trace principles to protect the natural beauty of the area.

**Booking and Equipment**

It is advisable to book paragliding experiences in advance, especially during peak tourist seasons. For mountain biking, consider renting equipment a day in advance to ensure availability and to get an early start on the trails.

Combining hiking with biking and paragliding in Zermatt offers a dynamic way to experience the Swiss Alps. This multidimensional approach not only enhances the adventure but also allows participants to appreciate the natural beauty from multiple perspectives. Whether you're pedaling through alpine meadows or soaring above them, Zermatt provides an unforgettable backdrop for an action-packed holiday.

## Other Adventure Activities in Zermatt: Skiing, Mountaineering, and Ski Touring

Nestled in the heart of the Swiss Alps, Zermatt is not just a picturesque mountain town but also a hub for some of the most exhilarating and challenging adventure activities in the world. Renowned for its skiing, mountaineering, and skitouring, Zermatt attracts enthusiasts from around the globe looking to test their limits against some of nature's most awe-inspiring backdrops.

### Skiing in Zermatt
### World-Class Ski Resorts

Zermatt is home to one of the largest ski resorts in the Alps, offering over 360 kilometers of pistes with varying degrees of difficulty. The resort is unique in that it provides year-round skiing, thanks to the Theodul Glacier, making it one of the few places in Europe where summer skiing is possible.

The ski areas around Zermatt are divided into four main sectors: Sunnegga, Gornergrat, Klein Matterhorn, and Schwarzsee. Each offers a distinct skiing experience:

Sunnegga is perfect for families and beginners, with gentle slopes and plenty of sunny days.
Gornergrat offers more challenging runs and spectacular views of the Matterhorn.

Klein Matterhorn serves as the gateway to the highest pistes and links to Italy's Breuil-Cervinia and Valtournenche. Schwarzsee provides challenging descents and is favored by more experienced skiers.

## Innovations and Sustainability
Zermatt is also at the forefront of sustainable ski resort operations, utilizing renewable energy sources extensively. The resort's lift systems are

powered by hydroelectricity, and efforts are continually made to reduce the carbon footprint of its operations.

## Mountaineering in Zermatt
The Alpine Challenge

Mountaineering is deeply embedded in the heritage of Zermatt. The town serves as the starting point for numerous high-alpine expeditions, including ascents of the Matterhorn—one of the most famous and challenging climbs in the world.

### Guided Tours and Safety

For those new to mountaineering or looking to tackle particularly tough peaks, Zermatt offers guided tours with experienced local guides. These professionals provide not only expertise and navigation but also education on high-altitude safety, weather considerations, and equipment use.

## Iconic Routes

Apart from the Matterhorn, other popular mountaineering challenges include:

Monte Rosa – the highest peak in Switzerland, offering various routes ranging from the relatively straightforward to the highly technical. Breithorn – considered one of the more accessible 4000-meter peaks, suitable for beginner mountaineers yet rewarding with stunning panoramic views.

## Ski Touring in Zermatt

Combining Skiing and Mountaineering

Ski Touring, or ski mountaineering, is an activity that combines skiing and hiking, allowing participants to ascend mountain slopes with skis equipped with special bindings and skins. Zermatt offers numerous ski touring routes that range from day trips to multi-day expeditions.

Popular Ski Touring Routes

Haute Route – Perhaps the most famous ski touring route in the world, the Haute Route from Zermatt to Chamonix crosses several mountain passes and glaciers and is a must-do for any serious ski mountaineer.

Schwarztor – This route is known for its long descents and stunning vistas, traversing glaciers and navigating through crevassed areas.

Ski Touring requires both skiing ability and mountaineering knowledge. Participants need to be well-prepared with the appropriate avalanche safety gear, including transceivers, probes, and shovels, and know how to use them. Local guides are highly recommended for those unfamiliar with the terrain or the intricacies of winter alpine navigation.

Zermatt offers a treasure trove of opportunities for those seeking adventure in the Alps. Each activity not only challenges the physical and mental prowess of its participants but also provides them with a deeper connection to the stunning natural environment of this iconic Swiss destination.

With state-of-the-art facilities, expert guidance available, and a strong commitment to sustainability, Zermatt continues to be a premier destination for skiing, mountaineering, and ski touring enthusiasts.

# SUSTAINABLE TOURISM PRACTICES

## Leaving No Trace: Eco-friendly Practices in Zermatt

Zermatt, renowned for its breathtaking landscapes and commitment to environmental stewardship, actively promotes eco-friendly practices that align with the "Leave No Trace" principles. These practices are essential in preserving the natural beauty and ecological integrity of this iconic Swiss mountain town and its surrounding areas. By adopting and promoting sustainable tourism, Zermatt ensures that it remains a pristine destination for future generations.

## Sustainable Transportation
Car-Free Village

One of the most significant eco-friendly practices in Zermatt is its status as a car-free village. Since 1961, the town has prohibited the use of combustion-engine vehicles within its limits, which helps maintain clean air and reduces environmental noise. Electric vehicles and horse-drawn carriages are common sights, providing sustainable and quaint alternatives for transportation around the town.

## Public Transport and Cable Cars

Zermatt invests heavily in its public transport systems, including electric buses and an extensive network of cable cars and cogwheel trains. These are not only efficient but also run on renewable energy sources, minimizing the carbon footprint associated with accessing the various mountain trails and ski areas.

**Energy and Resource Management**

Zermatt harnesses the power of hydroelectricity, which is abundant in the region due to its alpine rivers and lakes. This renewable energy source powers much of the town, including its public infrastructure, hotels, and restaurants, significantly reducing reliance on fossil fuels.

Water conservation is a priority in Zermatt, where the management of this precious resource is critical due to the seasonal flows of local water bodies. Measures are in place to ensure efficient water use in hotels, restaurants, and other facilities, which is essential in maintaining the ecological balance of the surrounding alpine environment.

**Waste Management**

Zermatt has a robust recycling and composting program, encouraging both residents and visitors to sort waste correctly to reduce landfill use and greenhouse gas emissions. There are numerous conveniently located recycling points throughout the town, and visitors are provided with clear instructions on how to dispose of recyclable and compostable waste properly.

The town encourages reduction in single-use plastics by promoting the use of reusable materials. Many shops and eateries offer sustainable alternatives, such as cloth shopping bags, reusable water bottles, and bamboo utensils, helping to decrease plastic waste that can harm the alpine environment.

## Protection of Natural Habitats

To protect the local flora and fauna, Zermatt meticulously manages its network of trails. Hiking and biking paths are regularly maintained to prevent erosion and minimize the impact on surrounding ecosystems. Information boards along these trails educate visitors about the sensitive alpine environment and the importance of staying on marked paths.

## Wildlife Conservation

Zermatt is home to diverse wildlife, including ibex, chamois, marmots, and eagles. The town, in collaboration with local conservation groups, implements measures to protect these species and their habitats. This includes regulating access to certain areas, particularly during sensitive times such as breeding seasons.

Zermatt invests in educational programs that teach visitors about the principles of Leave No Trace and the broader aspects of environmental conservation. Through guided tours, workshops, and information centers, tourists learn how their actions can impact the local environment and how they can help preserve it.

## Volunteer Initiatives

Several volunteer initiatives allow visitors to participate in local conservation efforts. These can include trail repair projects, clean-up days, and wildlife monitoring programs, providing hands-on opportunities to contribute positively to the environment.

Zermatt's commitment to eco-friendly practices and sustainable tourism is evident in every aspect of its operations and community ethos. By adhering to the Leave No Trace principles and actively promoting environmental stewardship, Zermatt not only protects its stunning alpine landscapes but also sets a standard for responsible tourism practices worldwide. These efforts ensure that visitors can enjoy the natural beauty of Zermatt responsibly and sustainably, preserving its magic for future generations.

## Conclusion

Zermatt, with its awe-inspiring landscapes and commitment to sustainability, serves as a model for responsible tourism. By integrating eco-friendly practices across transportation, energy consumption, waste management, and natural habitat protection, Zermatt ensures that its environmental footprint remains minimal while providing a high-quality experience for visitors. The town's proactive approach to sustainability not only preserves its stunning natural beauty but also enriches the visitor experience through educational initiatives and community engagement.

As a result, Zermatt not only offers a gateway to some of the most majestic scenery in the world but also leads by example in environmental stewardship, making it a prime destination for those who value both adventure and ecological responsibility. This commitment secures Zermatt's reputation as a top-tier destination for future generations of travelers, maintaining its status as a jewel in the crown of the Swiss Alps.

Printed in Dunstable, United Kingdom